CONSTRUCTING WALKING JAZZ BASS LINES BOOK II

WALKING BASS LINES
RHYTHM CHANGES IN 12 KEYS

A COMPLETE GUIDE TO CONSTRUCTING
WALKING BASS LINES

BASS TABLATURE EDITION

FOR THE

ELECTRIC
JAZZ BASSIST

BY
STEVEN MOONEY

© Waterfall Publishing House 2010

Special thanks to Jimmy Vass, Darcy Wright and Charlie Banacos
and to my wife Madoka for her constant love and support.

Copyright © WATERFALL PUBLISHING HOUSE 2010

This title is published by Waterfall Publishing House
Astoria, New York USA 11102

All Rights Reserved
No part of this publication may be produced, stored in a retrieval system or transmitted in any form or means, photocopying, mechanical or electronic without prior written permission of Waterfall Publishing House.

2nd printing September 2011

Print Edition ISBN 978-0-9829570-3-5
eBook   ISBN 978-0-9829570-7-3

Library of Congress Control Number: 2010938918

Japanese Print Edition ISBN 978-1-937147-19-4
Japanese eBook Edition ISBN 978-1-937147-20-0

Musical Score : Jazz
Musical Score : Studies & exercises, etudes

Layout and music engraving by Steven Mooney
Cover Design by Steven Mooney

© Waterfall Publishing House 2010

FOREWARD

Rhythm Changes like the " Blues " is an essential part of the Jazz musicians vocabulary.

Book II in the Constructing Walking Jazz Bass Lines series Rhythm Changes in 12 Keys provides various insights into how the Rhythm Changes song form may be approached by the Jazz Bassist.

Part I outlines the Rhythm Changes form and provides examples of how to construct walking jazz bass lines using voice leading, chromatic passing tones, pedal points, tri-tone substitutions, and harmonic anticipation.

Part II provides an in-depth look at the Rhythm Changes A sections and shows the common chord substitutions used by the bebop musicians when improvising.

Part III provides an in-depth look at the Bridge or B section providing various chord substitutions used when improvising and walking bass lines.

Part IV outlines Rhythm Changes in 12 keys using all the previous lesson topics and bass line examples outlined in the book.

Included are over 100 choruses of professional jazz bass lines in all 12 keys.
Suitable for the beginning to advanced electric bassist.

© Waterfall Publishing House 2010

TABLE OF CONTENTS

PART I

Rhythm Changes	p. 6
The AABA Form	p. 7
The AABA Structure in Digital Form	p. 9
Diatonic 7ths in the key of Bb major	p. 11
The "2" feel	p. 12
Embellishing the "2" feel	p. 13
The Dominant 7th chord and voice leading	p. 16
Applying the Dominant 7th voice leading technique to jazz bass lines	p. 17
Chromatic approach from below	p. 19
Chromatic approach from above	p. 20
Chromaticism and the walk up and the walk down	p. 22
Repeated notes and chromaticism	p. 25
Harmonic anticipation and playing across the bar line	p. 27
Voice leading and 7th chords	p. 29
Applying the 7th chord voice leading technique to jazz bass lines	p. 30
Pedal points	p. 31
Tri-Tone substitution	p. 33
Expanding on the use of Tri-Tone substitution	p. 34
The Turnaround	p. 35
Turnarounds and the AABA Form	p. 37

PART II

Rhythm Changes the "A" section progressions	p. 39

© Waterfall Publishing House 2010

TABLE OF CONTENTS   cont.

PART III
Rhythm Changes the Bridge .... p. 61
Secondary Dominant Chords .... p. 62
Rhythm Changes the Bridge chord substitutions .... p. 63

PART IV
Rhythm Changes in 12 Keys
Rhythm Changes in Bb .... p. 69
Rhythm Changes in B .... p. 80
Rhythm Changes in C .... p. 88
Rhythm Changes in Db .... p. 96
Rhythm Changes in D .... p. 104
Rhythm Changes in Eb .... p. 112
Rhythm Changes in E .... p. 120
Rhythm Changes in F .... p. 128
Rhythm Changes in Gb .... p. 136
Rhythm Changes in G .... p. 144
Rhtyhm Changes in Ab .... p. 152
Rhythm Changes in A .... p. 160

In Conclusion .... p. 168

© Waterfall Publishing House 2010

RHYTHM CHANGES

Rhythm Changes like the " Blues " is an essential part of the Jazz musicians vocabulary. The following chapters provide various insights into how the Rhythm Changes song form may be approached.

It is essential for the aspiring bassist to learn the following material in all 12 keys as layed out in the following chapters. It is then advised that the student take the various lines and devices and build their own bass lines by substituting various A section or B section bass lines from the examples within.

Write the lines out on manuscript.
This will enable the student to compose and hear their own bass melodies and to accelerate the process of becoming a Jazz Bassist in their own right.

It is essential for the Jazz Bassist to have a strong understanding of the harmony of the music being played, a solid rhythmic foundation but most importantly to have their own sound and identity.

Enjoy the book.

© Waterfall Publishing House 2010

PART I RHYTHM CHANGES - THE AABA FORM

The following exercise outlines the form and chord changes to Rhythm Changes in the key of Bb.
By form we mean the structure of the tune. Rhythm Changes like many jazz standard song forms consists of 32 bars and the following AABA structure.
Eg.   1st A - 8 bars ,   2nd A - 8 bars ,   Bridge or B - 8 bars,   Last A - 8 bars

THE AABA STRUCTURE IN DIGITAL FORM

The following example outlines the Rhythm Changes song form with the use of *Digitals*, or *Roman Numerals*.

The use of *Digitals* is commonly referred to in jazz as an accurate and time saving method to describe a chord structure or melody line. The refference comes from the diatonic chord structure, or the scale degrees.

In the following example we have the regular chord changes above the staff and the related *Roman Numerals* below.

© Waterfall Publishing House 2010

In the Bridge or B section you will notice a series of dominant 7th chords, this cycle is known as a V of V cycle, consisting of a series of secondary dominant chords. This will be discussed in greater detail in the Bridges chapter on page 62.

DIATONIC 7ths IN THE KEY OF Bb Major

The following example outlines the diatonic 7th chords built off of the Bb major scale. Knowing how to build the diatonic 7th chords will help the bassist to understand how the *Digital* and *Roman Numeral* system is used.

In the 1st example we have the Bb major scale.
The 2nd example shows the diatonic 7th chords built from the Bb major scale.
The diatonic 7th chords are built in thirds off of the scale .
We build the chord by starting at the root note and moving up a third or 2 steps in the scale.

For example to build Bb major 7 we have the notes Bb D F A
to build Cminor 7 we have C Eb G Bb etc.

Bb major scale

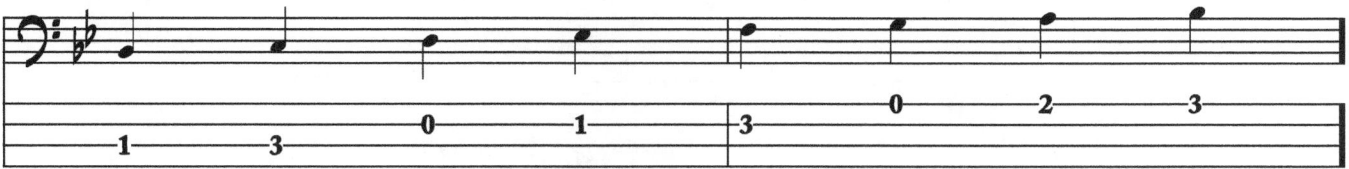

Diatonic 7th chords built from the Bb major scale.

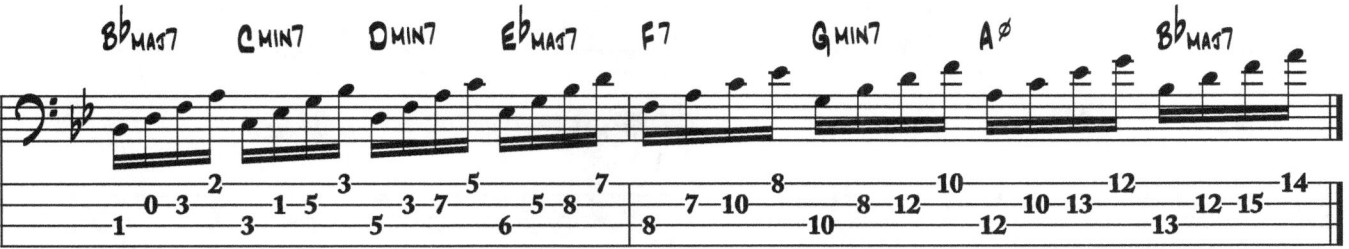

Roman Numeral / Digital System.

By reviewing the above examples we can now look back at the A A B A structure in *Digital* form and understand what is happening.
Having a working knowledge of the diatonic chord structures helps the bassist to analyse tunes on the spot and determine the key of a tune or chord sequence.

© Waterfall Publishing House 2010

THE " 2 " FEEL

The following exercise outlines Rhythm Changes in the key of Bb demonstrating a fundamental bass line using the " 2 " feel. The " 2 " feel is generally played on the head and opening choruses of the solo. This enables the band and soloist to build momentum throughout the tune. The " 2 " feel bass line Ex. below is constructed using the chord tones (1, 3, 5) known as the triad.

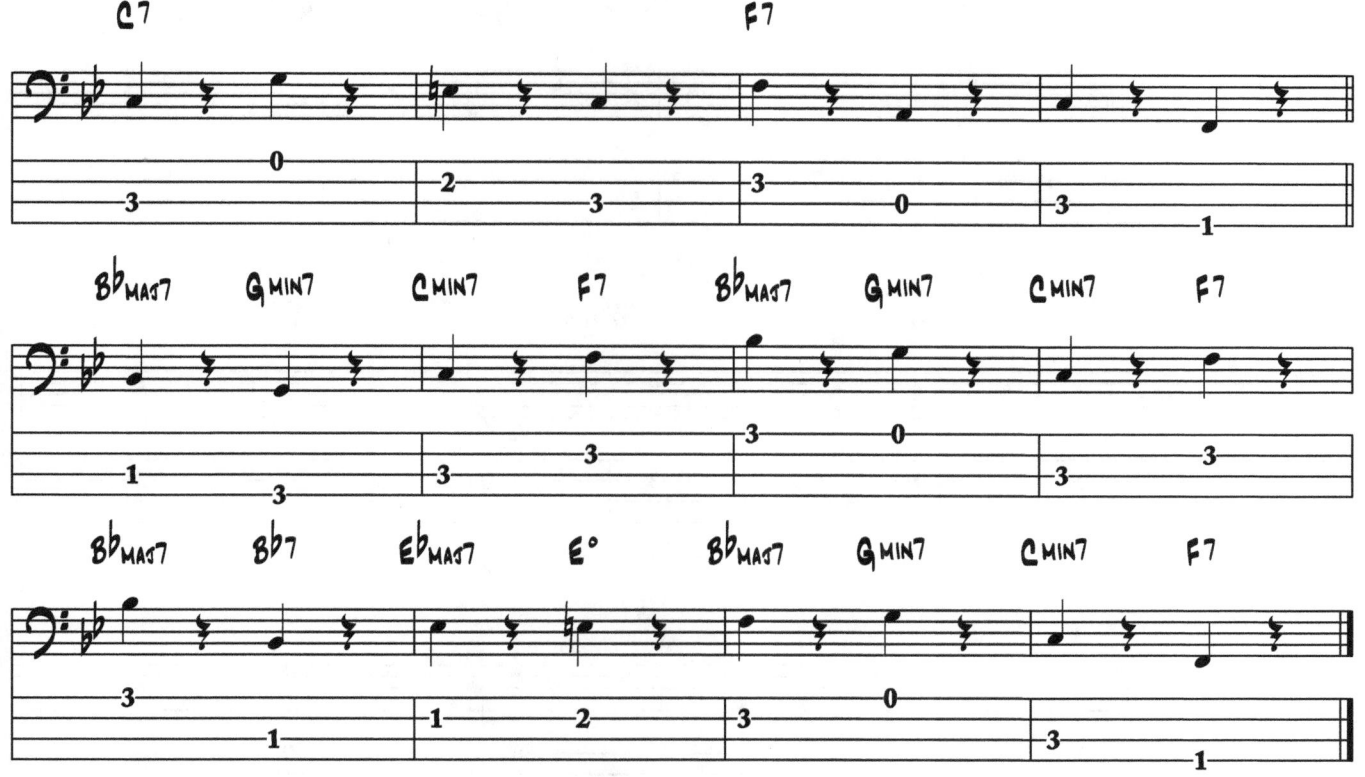

EMBELLISHING THE " 2 " FEEL

In the following example we incorporate rhythmic phrasing into the bass line designed to propel the music forward and make the bass line more rhythmically interesting. Breaking up the " 2 " feel in this way helps to build the transition into the " 4 " feel.

When breaking up the line as shown in Ex. 2 the main objective is to be supporting the melody or soloist at all times. Laying the foundation.

Notice in the last 4 bars of the final chorus of this exercise we hint that the " 4 " feel is coming in the next chorus.

© Waterfall Publishing House 2010

THE DOMINANT 7th CHORD & VOICE LEADING

The following example outlines Rhythm Changes in Bb using a " 4" feel.
In this example we are using triads (chord tones 1, 3, 5) to construct our walking bass line.
We will apply a voice leading technique in the 4th & 5th bar of the " A " section and also apply the same technique in the Bridge or " B " section of this exercise.
Here the b7th of the Dom7 chord will resolve up a whole step or down a half step to a chord tone of the next chord . When voice leading the Dom7th chord we add 1 note to the triad, the b7th. We use chord tones (1, 3, 5, b7) eg the 7th chord.

Ex.1 Here the Eb the b7th of the F7 moves down a half step to the D the 3rd of Bbmaj7

Ex.2 Here the Eb the b7th of the F7 moves up a whole step too the F the 5th of Bbmaj7

© Waterfall Publishing House 2010

Ex.3 Here the Ab the b7th of the Bb7 moves down a half step to the G the 3rd of Ebmaj7

Ex.4 Here the F the b7th of the G7 moves down a half step to the E the 3rd of C7

APPLYING THE DOMINANT 7th VOICE LEADING TECHNIQUE TO JAZZ BASS LINES

The following chorus of Rhythm Changes in Bb major outlines the voice leading technique applied to the Dominant 7th chord.

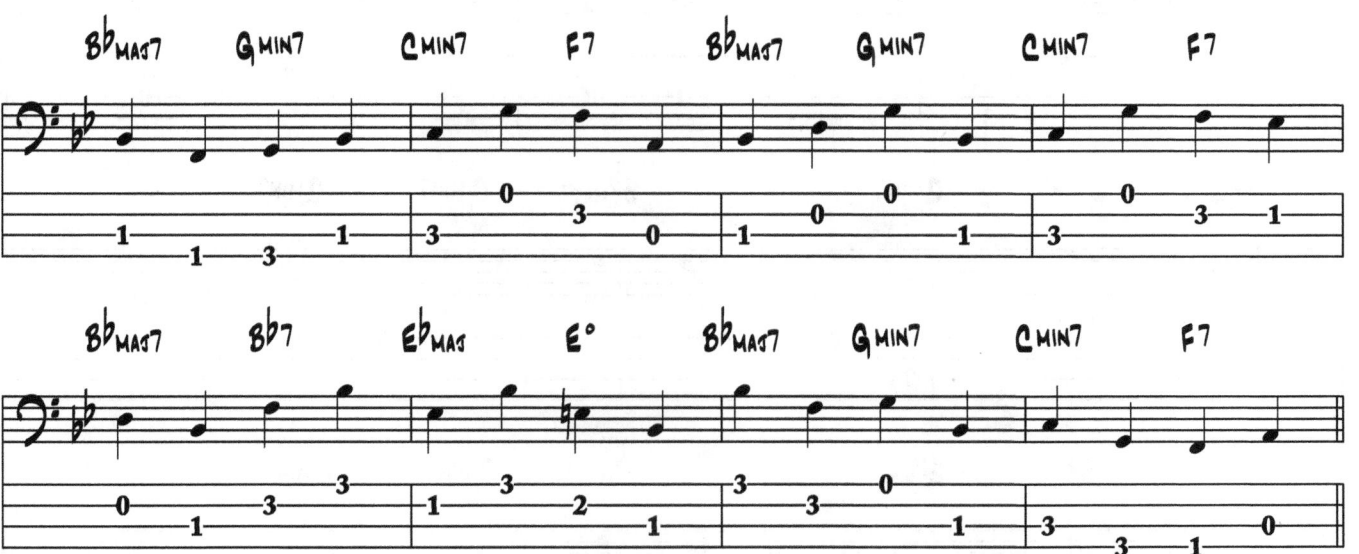

THE CHROMATIC APPROACH FROM BELOW

In the following example we use the device known as the chromatic approach note. Here we use the approach note a half step below the chord tone. This is a very effective technique used to give the line contour and a distinctive sound.

The application of the chromatic approach note and other devices is what gives a particular player " their own sound " this is what all good bassists are striving for.

© Waterfall Publishing House 2010

THE CHROMATIC APPROACH FROM ABOVE

The following example continues the previous application of the use of the chromatic approach note. This time we use the approach note from a half step above the chord tone. As in the previous example the approach notes are very effective when used correctly. When overdone the approach notes tend to lose their effectiveness. As a general rule when starting to apply the chromatic approaches use the chord tones on beat 1 & 3 and chromatic approaches on beats 2 & 4. As you become more adept you will find that the contour and direction of the line will dictate where the approach notes fall.

© Waterfall Publishing House 2010

CHROMATICISM .... THE WALK UP & THE WALK DOWN

In the following example we continue our approach to chromaticism with two commonly used devices in jazz bass playing. The walk up connects to the next chord by walking up to the next chord change with two chromatic approach notes. The walk down connects to the next chord change with two chromatic approaches walking down. This is very strong bass line motion and gives a definite sense of where the line is going.

THE WALK DOWN.....

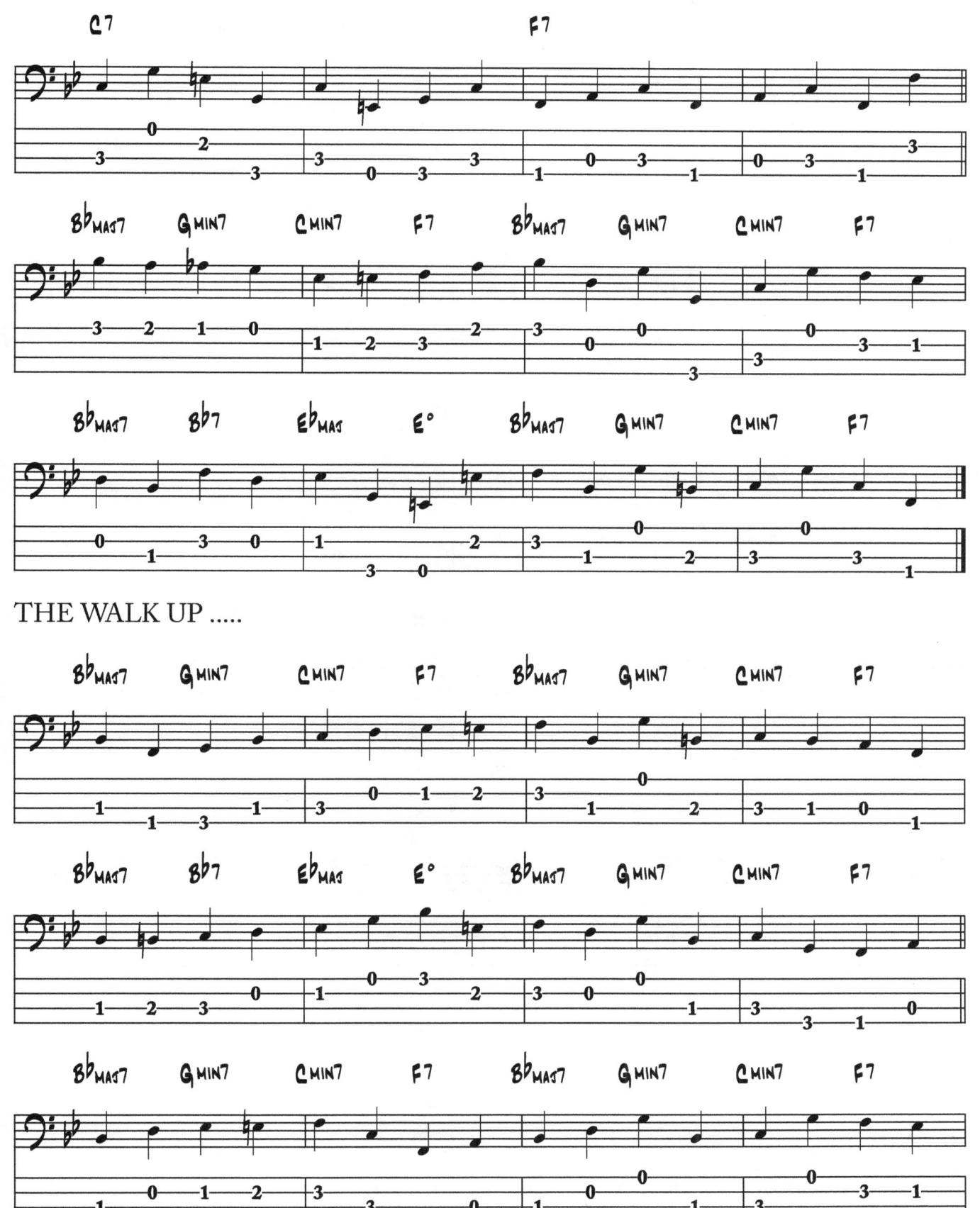

THE WALK UP .....

REPEATED NOTES AND CHROMATICISM

In the following example we combine our look at chromaticism with the device of repeated notes. Repeated notes are very effective when the harmonic rhythm increases, eg. two chords per bar. Repeated notes were used extensively in the bebop era as the chord structures developed into two or four chords per bar.

The repeated notes give a strong sense of the harmony being outlined and gives a strong sense of forward motion.

© Waterfall Publishing House 2010

HARMONIC ANTICIPATION & PLAYING ACROSS THE BAR

In the following example we look at the technique known as playing across the bar or playing ahead of the changes. The harmony is played for example 1 beat or 1/2 beat early and tied across the bar line. Using this device the tied note is sounded once and sustained over the bar line. This is another device which gives the bass line a strong sense of forward motion. When incorporating this technique into bass lines the most important factor to be considered is, am I supporting the melody or soloist and providing a strong foundation.

VOICE LEADING AND 7th CHORDS

In the following example we incorporate 7th chords into our bass line and a technique known as voice leading. Voice leading is a very effective technique used by all harmonic instruments. Voice leading is a method where a chord tone resolves stepwise to another chord tone of the next chord change. This provides very strong lines and can help to connect the bassist to the piano voicings. Soloists often use this method when constructing guide tone lines.

Ex. 1 Here the Bb the b7th of Cmin7 moves down a half step and resolves to the
A the 3rd of F7 in this II V I progression

Ex. 2 Here the Eb the b7th of F7 resolves down a half step to the D the 3rd of
Bb maj

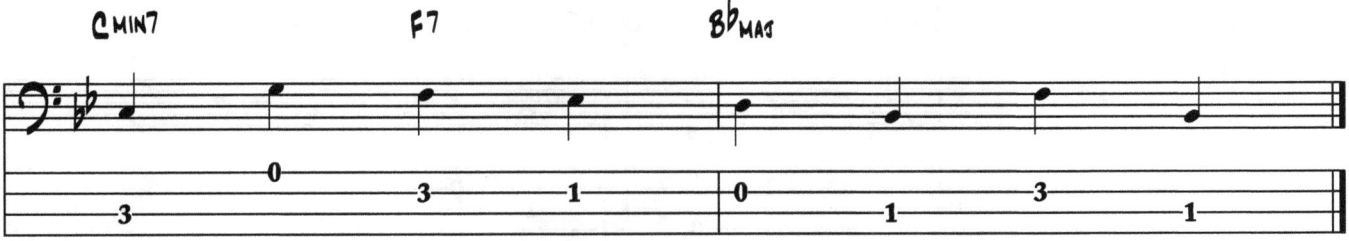

The following chorus of Rhythm Changes in Bb major outlines the voice leading technique applied to the 7th chords.

© Waterfall Publishing House 2010

APPLYING THE 7th CHORDS VOICE LEADING TECHNIQUE TO JAZZ BASS LINES

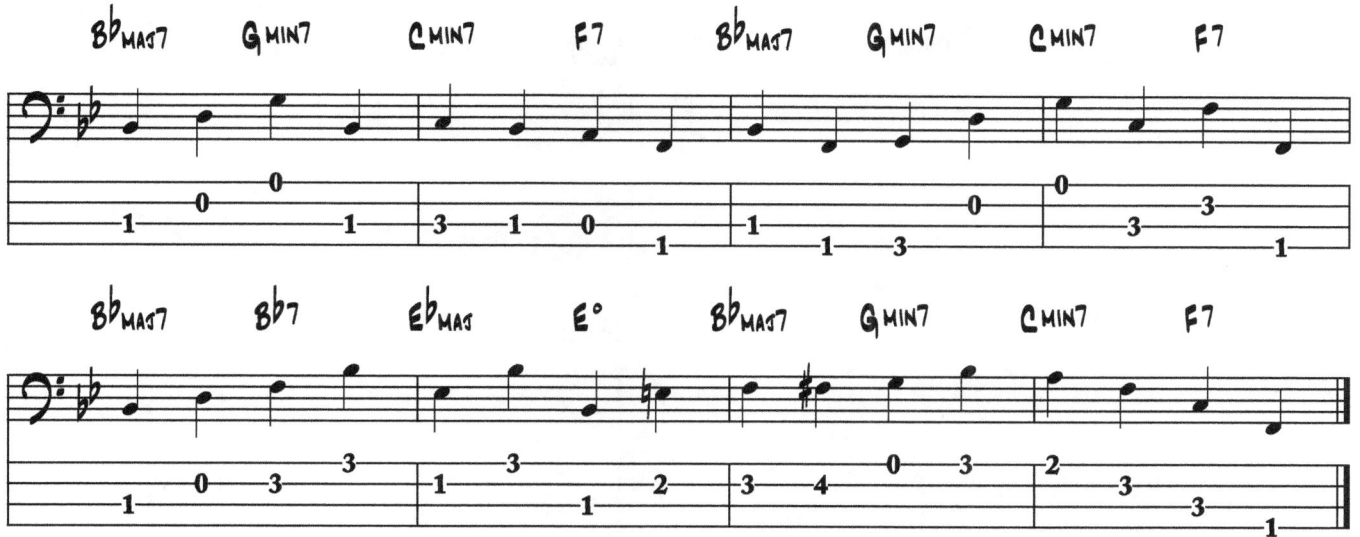

PEDAL POINTS

In the following example we look at the technique known as the pedal point.
There are various types of pedal points, the repeated note for an extended number of beats or measures and the rhythmic pedal point.
The pedal point is a device often used to start a tune eg. you might here a horn player say play a pedal on the V chord. A common pedal played in jazz is a pedal on 2 & 4, although there are many types.
Another use of the pedal point is to create tension or a feeling of suspension as one bass note is played throughout a progression of chords, then when the pedal tone is released and the bass goes into walking the changes the tension is released and the music propels forward.
This gives the listener the sense that the band is really cookin'.

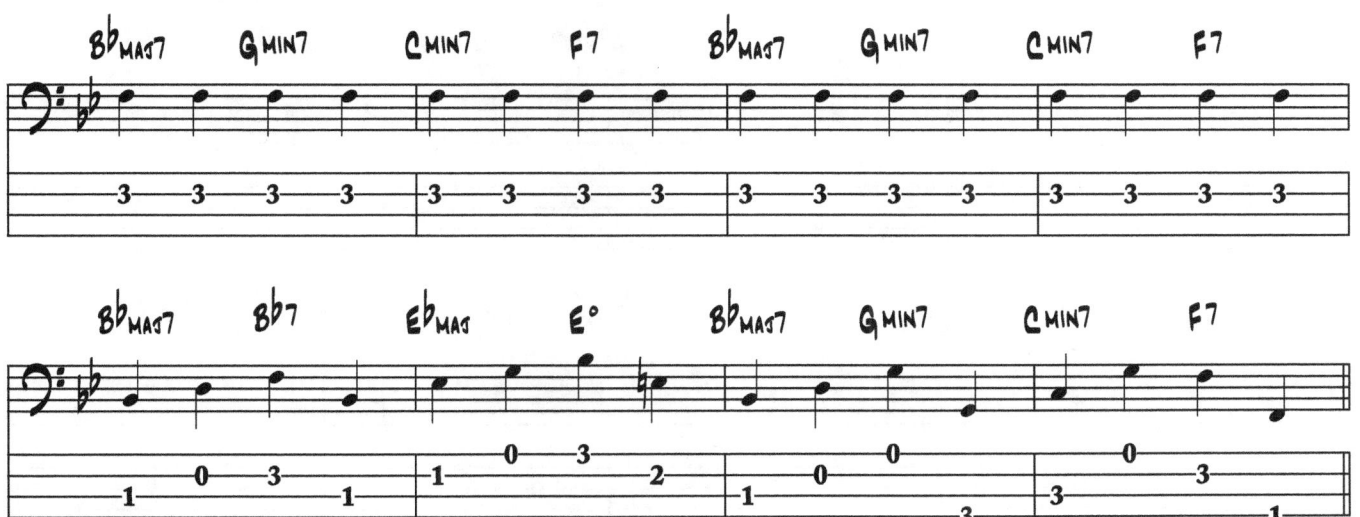

TRI TONE SUBSTITUTION

In the following examples we will examine the harmonic technique known as the tri tone substitute.
The tri tone substitute is used in various ways.
The first use is to make different chord tensions against the melody note which may make the melody note sound more interesting or create a different mood.
   This is down to personal taste. A great melody is a great melody by itself, this is why tunes become " standards ".
The other use of the tri tone substitute is to create chromatic root movement, therefore creating very strong forward motion.

The term tri tone comes from the substitute note being three tones or whole steps away from the root note.
In the following example we start at F the root note and move 3 tones or whole steps, which brings us to B natural, the interval of a tritone.

Ex. In the following example we have the F7 chord followed by the tritone substitute B7.
 A dominant 7 chord can be voiced by playing only the two notes of the tritone interval eg. A and Eb. This sound is identifiable as the dominant 7 sound because the interval of a tritone is unique to the Dom7 chord. There is no interval of a tritone in major or minor chords without extensions. What this means is if we look at the example below and play the common tones from both chords, the A and the Eb we have essentially the same sound using different chords.

Note that the Eb and D# are enharmonically the same note.

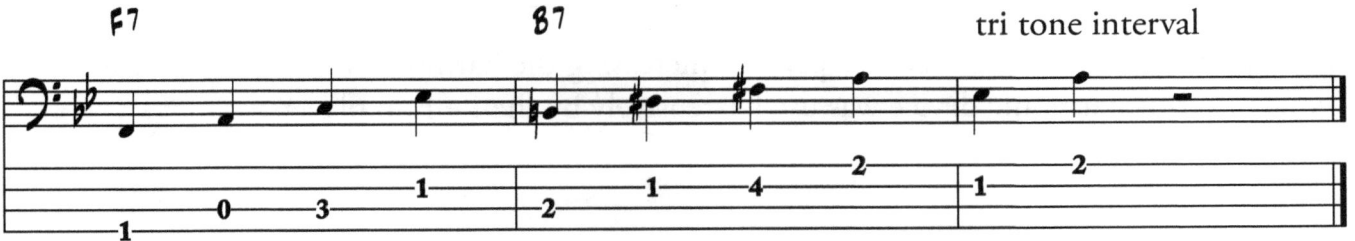

© Waterfall Publishing House 2010

EXPANDING ON THE USE OF TRI TONE SUBSTITUTION

In the following examples we will look at the use of tri tone substitution related to constructing bass lines with chromatic root movement.
In the following example we have the II V progression in the key of Bb major
eg   Cmin7 F7   would resolve to Bb major.

In the next example we apply the tri tone substitution to the Cmin7 F7 - Bbmaj chord progression. Then we have the following progression Cmin7 B7 - Bbmaj
Here the root of the chords is moving down chromatically or by semi tones.

Following on from the last example we will now add the relative IImin7 to the tri tone substitute. Note this is where understanding the diatonic 7ths and the *Digital /Roman Numeral* system really pays off.
The relative IImin7 of the tri tone B7 is F# min7.
The new chord progression is as follows.

The 2nd measure now has 2 chords per bar, increasing the harmonic rhythm of the chord sequence. This harmonic device was used extensively by the Be Bop players.

In the next example we continue the device of increasing the harmonic rhythm by applying the original II V Cmin7 F7 before the tri tone substitution.
The progression is as follows.

The use of tri tone substitution and increasing the harmonic rhythm has a distinctive sound. Again this is down to personal taste.
The use of these and other harmonic devices should be used in context with the music being played.
The bassists role in a jazz context is to lay a solid foundation, with swinging lines that outline the harmony and makes the soloist or melody sound good. This is the key to being a working musician.

THE TURNAROUND

In the following examples we look at the " turnaround ". The turnaround refers to the last 2 bars of the chord progression which leads us back to the top of the form. Quite often you might here someone on the bandstand say, " turn it around " this means start the next tune on the turnaround. Like the pedal point intro, the turnaround intro is very common and can be extended indefinately until the melody comes in.

The most common turnaround is the I VI II V progression, here it is in relation to Rhythm changes in Bb.

© Waterfall Publishing House 2010

In the following example we substitute the I chord for the III chord, now we have the progression as follows. Notice in this example the Vi chord is a Dominant 7th chord. This is because it is functioning as a Secondary Dominant chord eg. V of I eg G7 - Cm7.

In the following example we apply the tritone substitutes to our turnaround, the progression is as follows. By applying the tritone subsitutes we now have chromatic root movement.

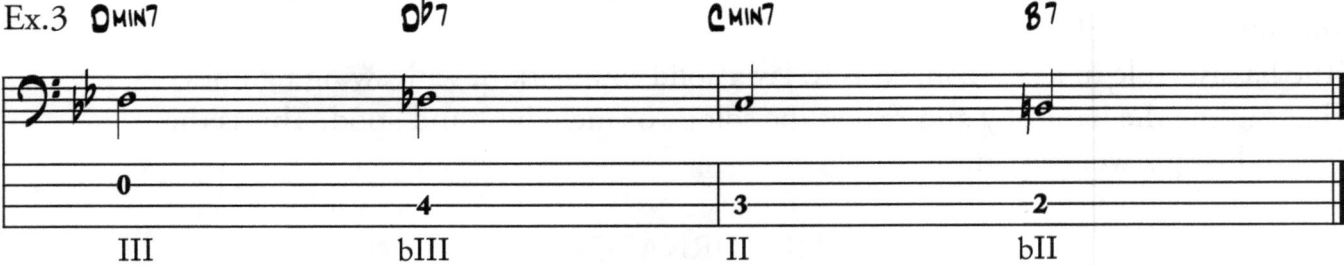

By revising the last chapter we can add greater harmonic rhythm to the turnaround by using the relative IImin7 chord to the tri tone sub.
The following progression would look like this.

© Waterfall Publishing House 2010

TURNAROUNDS & THE AABA FORM

In the previous chapter we looked at the turnaround and some of the variations which can be used.

The AABA form presents the bassist with another challenge related to the turnaround.

The 1st A section has a turnaround going back to Bb maj in the following example we use the III VI II V turnaround.

Moving to the 2nd A you will notice the turnaround is I V I. This is because the tune resolves before moving to another part of the form. The bridge contains another harmonic structure, this happens regularly in the AABA form.

Before moving to the next section the 2nd A must be completed, eg resolved.

Its like finishing a chapter in a story before you start the next one.

In the Last A the turnaround is taking us back to the top of the tune or back to the start eg the original key, here we use the I VI II V progression or any of its substitutes. The following chorus of Rhythm Changes in Bb outlines the previous examples.

PART II RHYTHM CHANGES THE " A " SECTION
PROGRESSIONS

In the following examples we look at various chord progressions found in the " A " section of Rhythm Changes. The first chorus uses the basic " 2 " feel followed by the " 4 " feel in the second chorus in each example.
Rhythm Changes form is A A B A . With the first " A " having a slight variation from the second " A ", this is due to the second " A " resolving before going to the " B " section or bridge.
We will look at some of the common progressions which can be combined together when playing behind the soloist to keep the music moving in different directions. Rhythm Changes is often played at fast tempos , and having the various chord progressions and available substitutes under ones fingers is a valuable asset for any aspiring bassist to have.
The following examples are played almost entirely in the bottom register of the instrument using predominantly triads and combine some of the previous devices mentioned in Part 1 of this book.
It is a valuable skill to be able to walk the changes to Rhythm Changes or any other tune for that matter in the bottom register of the instrument. This gives depth or bottom to the sound of the band. Being able to play any tune without having to shift more than a half step from the open position makes fast tempo issues easier to come to terms with.
We will take an indepth look at the various devices covering the whole register of the instrument in the second part of this book.

© Waterfall Publishing House 2010

Ex.5

PART III   RHYTHM CHANGES " THE BRIDGE "

In the following chapter we look at the " Bridge " or " B " section of Rhythm Changes and some of the the possible variations used.

After reviewing the material in this chapter, it is recommended that the bassist revise the previous chapter and insert the " Bridge " substitutions into the previous examples of the " A " sections.

It is suggested to write the combinations out on manuscript paper and include them into the practice routine.

This will begin to give the bassist more variation and the ability to hear more complex bass line movement, the ability to substitute chords on the fly is a sought after skill and enables the bassist to suggest alternate harmonies for the soloist.

Various examples and combinations will be covered in the final chapter of this book when we look at Rhythm Changes in 12 keys.

SECONDARY DOMINANT CHORDS

The term Secondary Dominant is a term used regularly in jazz theory and harmony. The following example shows the application of the V of V cycle as it appears in the Rhythm Changes bridge.

In the key of Bb by refering to our original diatonic 7ths chart we know that the min7 chords are Cmin7, Dmin7, & Gmin7. The minor 7th chords can also be made dominant, this is known as a Secondary Dominant chord.

Therefore our Secondary Dominants chords in the key of Bb major are C7, D7, G7. By refering to the diatonic 7ths chart we know that the dominant 7th chord is the V chord. By looking at the example below of the Rhythm Changes Bridge in the key of Bb we see the V of V cycle.

eg. D is the 5th note of the G7 - V of V7
    G is the 5th note of the C7 - V of V7
    C is the 5th note of the F7 - V of V7
    F7 is the V chord in the key of Bb

Therefore the Bridge outlines the V of V cycle using Secondary Dominant chords modulating by a 5th until we get to F7 , F7 is not a Secondary Dominant F7 is the V chord of Bb major.

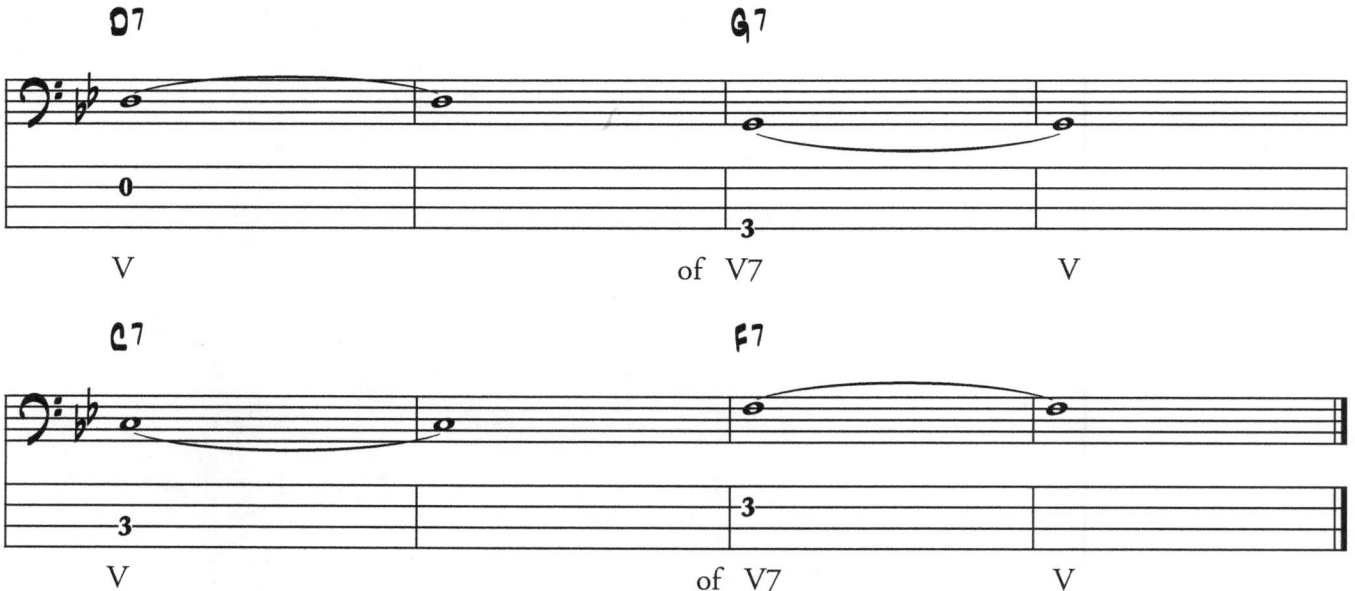

This is where the V of V terminology comes from, normally a Dom7 chord resolves to the tonic eg, F7 resolves to Bbmaj.

By using Secondary Dominant chords we can arrive at the V of V cycle where the Dom7 chord resolves to another Dom7 chord, because the Dom7 chord wants to resolve, by cycling around to another Dom7 chord it builds tension until the cycle finally resolves to a major chord. The Rhythm Changes Bridge is a classic example of the V of V cycle.

© Waterfall Publishing House 2010

RHYTHM CHANGES - THE BRIDGE CHORD SUBSTITUTIONS

Example 1. Here the B section outlines the previous V of V cycle using the relative IImin7 chord eg, Amin7 D7, Dmin7 G7 etc.
Again it is worth the effort to really understand the diatonic 7ths and the Digital references, enabling the bassist to quickly identify and understand the relationship between the chords in various progressions.

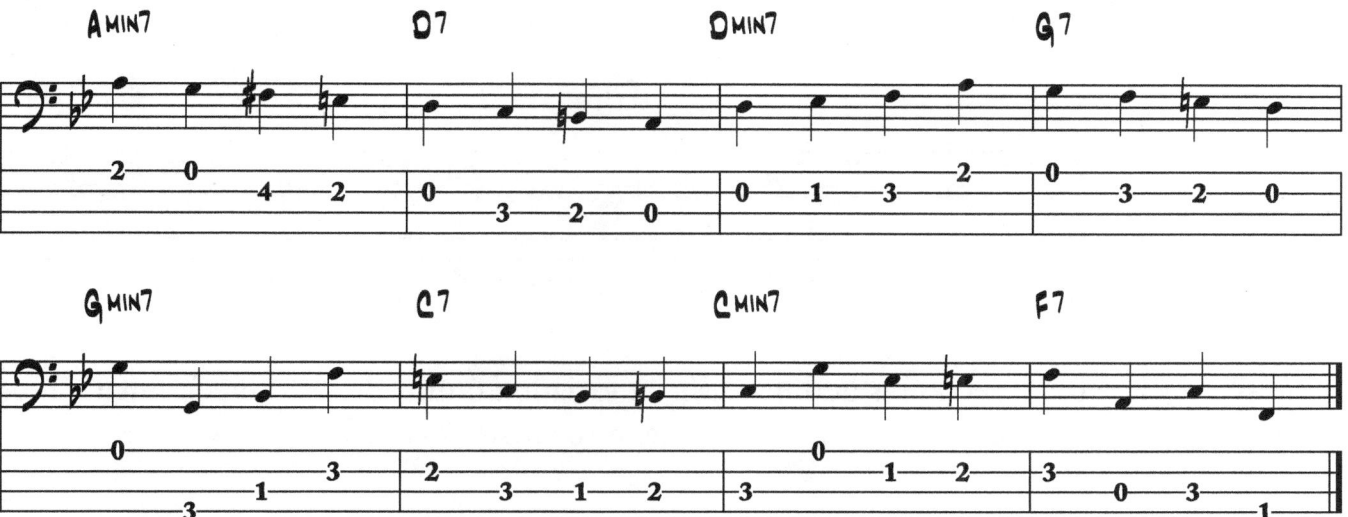

Example 2. Here the B section outlines the V of V cycle using the tritone substitutes, resulting in a descending chromatic root movement.

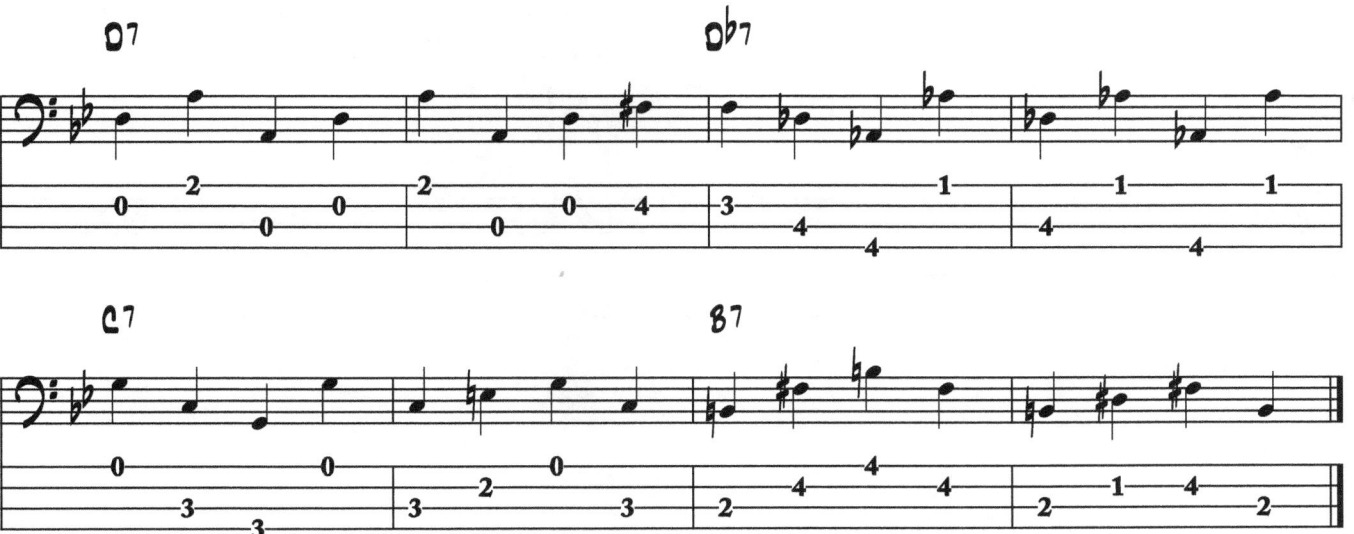

© Waterfall Publishing House 2010

Example 3. Here the B section outlines descending chromatic root movement eg. tritone substitutes, with the relative IImin7 chords.

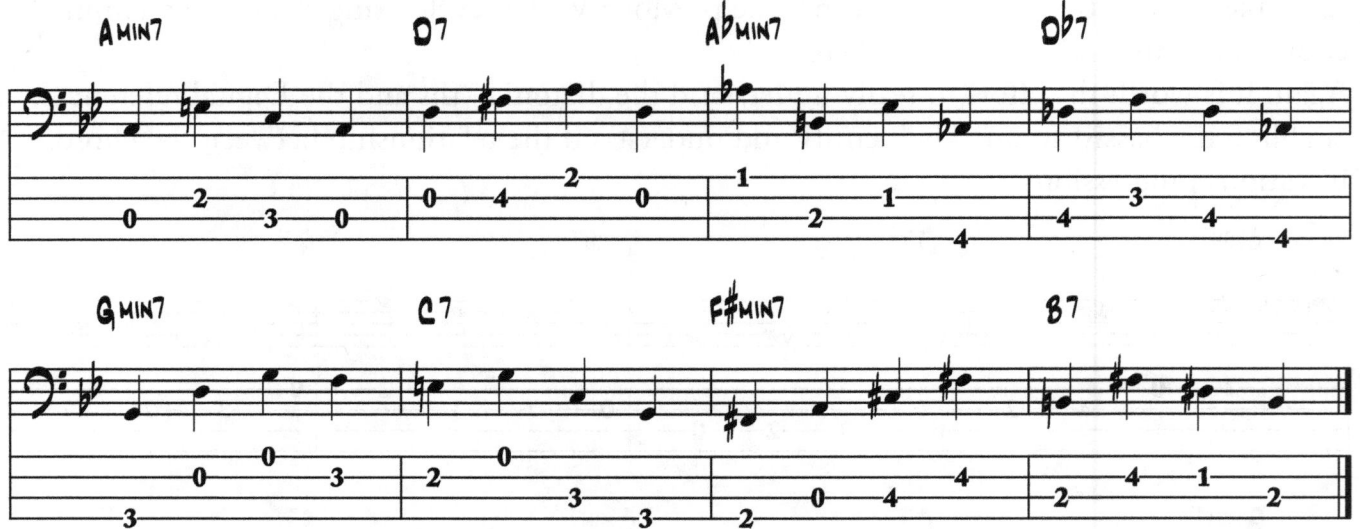

Example 4. Here the B section is outlined using a variation on the descending chromatic root movement, this time using the tritone substitute in the first measure eg. Ab7 is the tritone substitute of D7.

Example 5. Here the B section is outlined using the above descending chromatic root movement with the relative IImin7 chord.

Example 6. Here the B section uses another variation on the tritone substitutes, this B section increases the harmonic rhythm eg. increasing the no. of chords per bar. Notice in the 2nd measure we use the tritone substitute of D7 with the relative IImin7 chord eg. Ebmin7 Ab7.

© Waterfall Publishing House 2010

Example 7. Here we continue increasing the harmonic rhythm to example 7 now we have the relative IImin7 throughout the B section.

Example 8. Here we have a series of II V progressions , if we look at the last 4 measures of the B section you will notice the descending chromatic root movement and the increased harmonic rhythm, the tritone substitutes with the relative IImin7 chords.
The first 4 bars of the bridge are descending chromatic II V progressions. The complete B section therefore is a series of descending chromatic II V chord progessions.

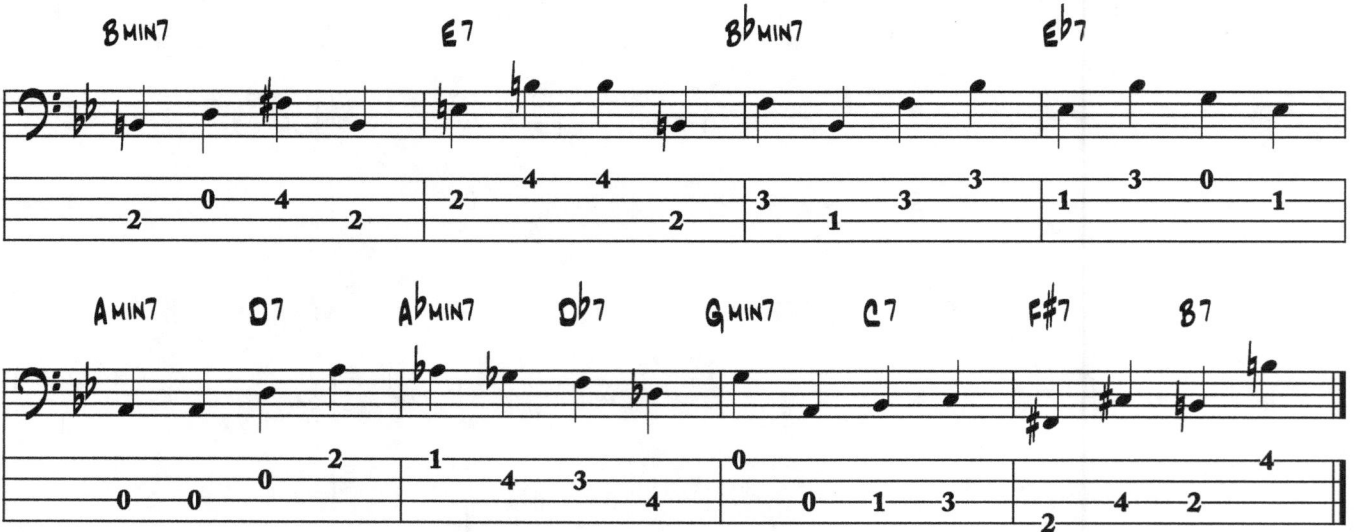

Example 9. Here the B section modulates to the IV chord eg. Ebmaj, this is a very common cycle in the jazz standard vocabulary. The progression sounds like a II V I III VI II V in Eb, however it is deceptive, the last II V is a II V leading back to the Tonic Bb major. The last 4 measures in this B section is the V of V cycle with the relative IImin7 chord.

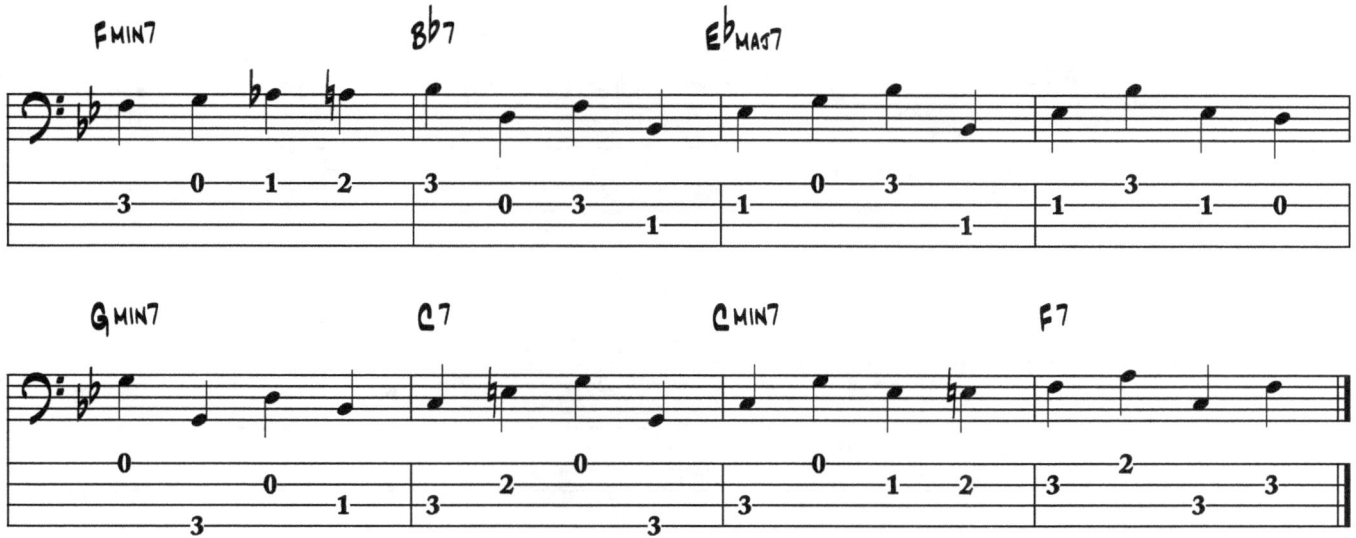

Example 10. Here the B section modulates up a 4th , we have a variation on the A section this time in the key of Eb major, eg up a 4th from the Tonic key of Bb major.

Example 11. Here the B section outlines the Diminished Cycle eg a cycle of minor 3rds. Notice that the first chord is the tritone substitute of the original B section chord D7. From here we cycle around in minor 3rds with the F7 bringing us back to Bb major.

Example 12. Here the B section once again outlines the Diminished Cycle this time incorporating the relative IImin7 into the progression.

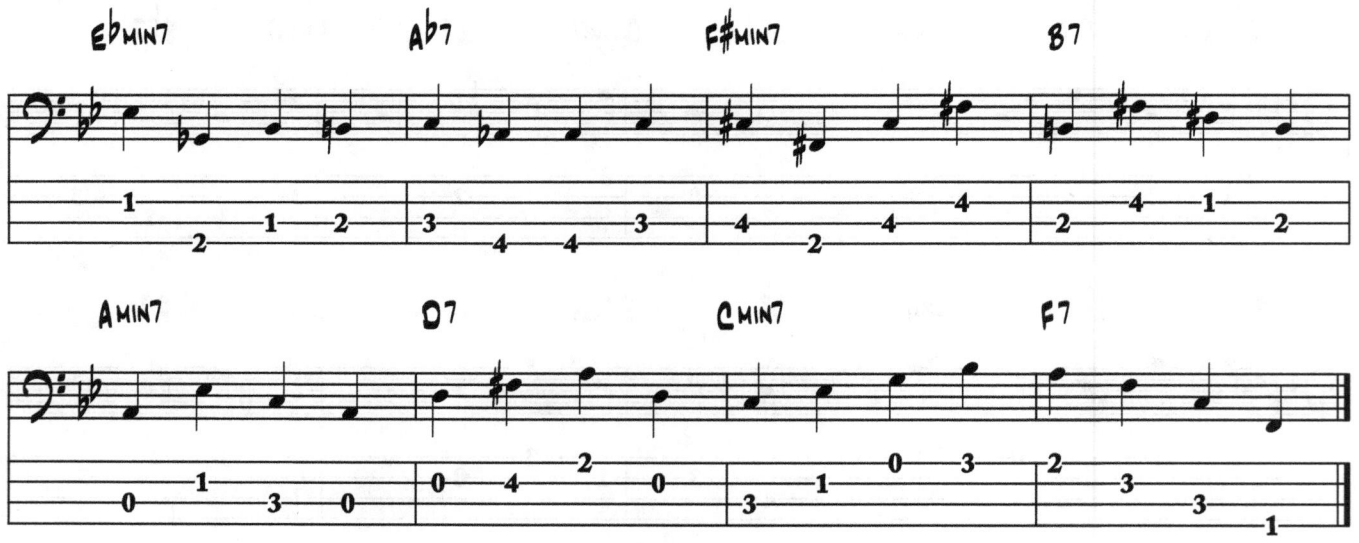

PART IV   RHYTHM CHANGES IN 12 KEYS

In the remaining pages we take an in depth look at the various lines and chord substitutions outlined in Part 1.

The following lines on Rhythm Changes cover the full range of the instrument, however never losing the functioning principle of the bass in this setting. To lay the foundation by outlining the changes and giving harmonic and rhythmic support to the soloist and or melody.

The following chapter is a study of Rhythm Changes in 12 keys using the chord progressions outlined in the previous chapters.

© Waterfall Publishing House 2010

73

RHYTHM CHANGES IN B

RHYTHM CHANGES IN C

RHYTHM CHANGES IN D

RHYTHM CHANGES IN Eb

RHYTHM CHANGES IN E

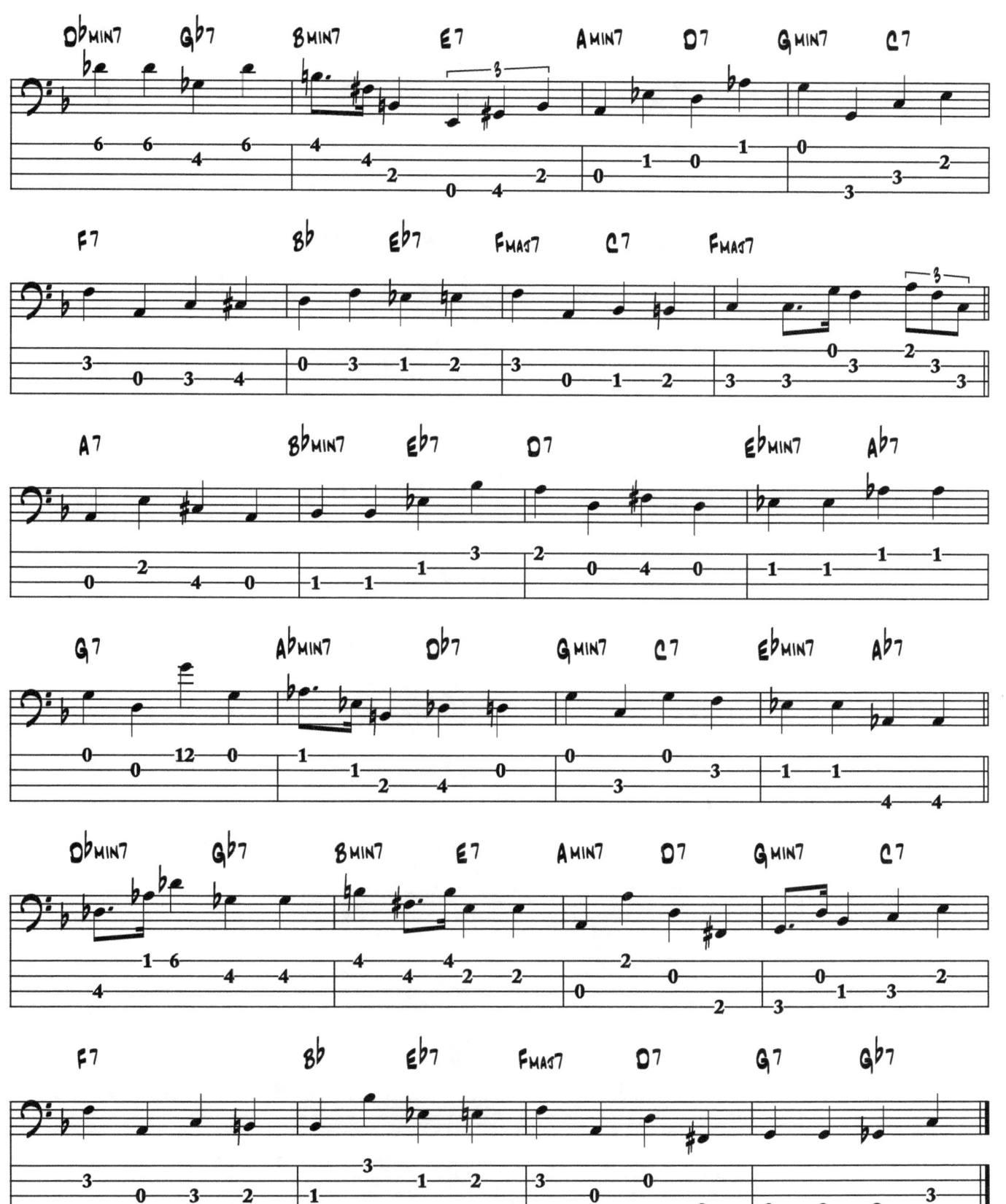

RHYTHM CHANGES IN Gb

RHYTHM CHANGES IN G

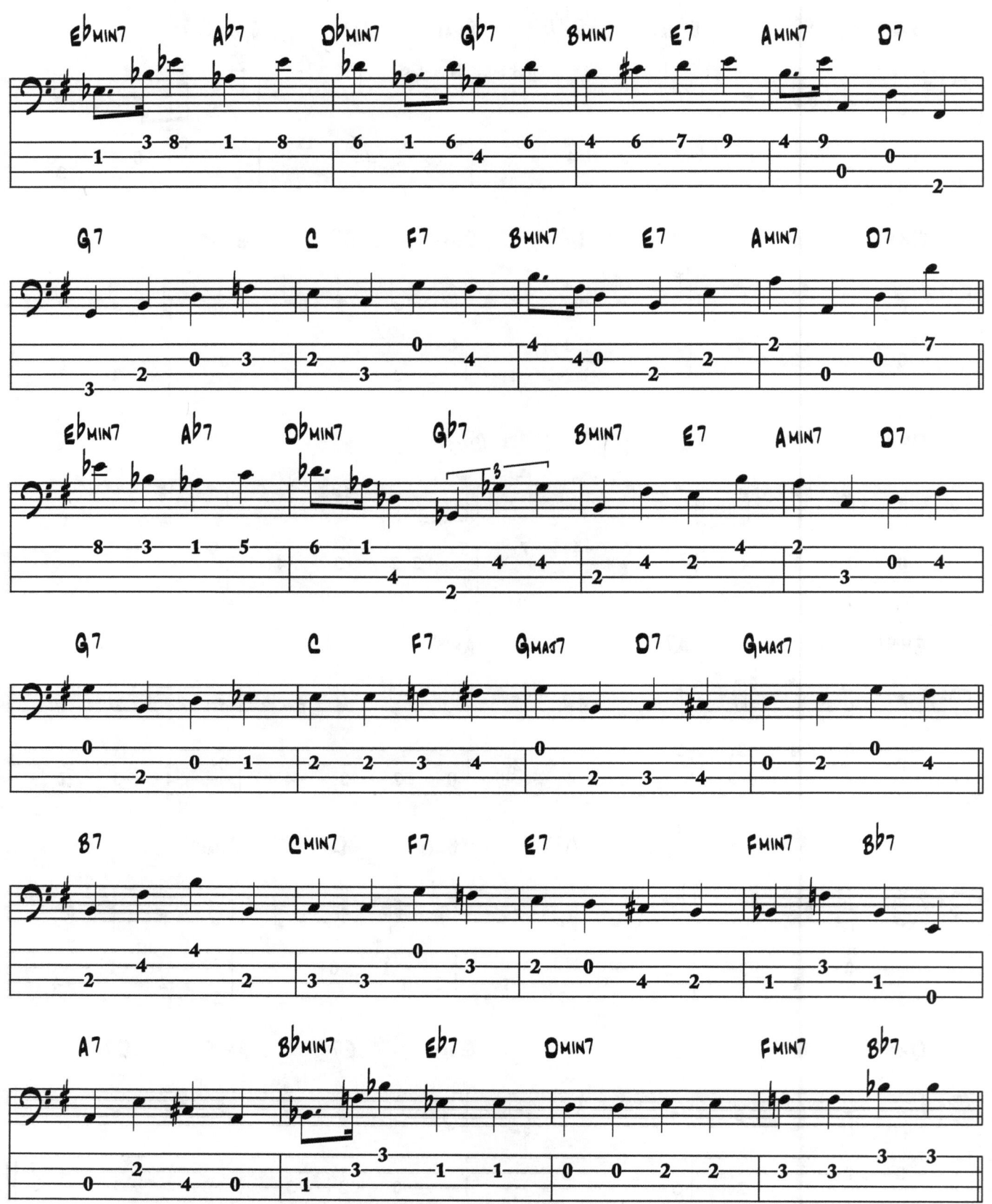

RHYTHM CHANGES IN Ab

RHYTHM CHANGES IN A

IN CONCLUSION ......
It has been a vast amount of work and dedicated practice that brings the bassist to the last page of this book having covered all the examples within.

It has been the aim of this book to give the aspiring bassist a solid grounding in understanding how to construct walking jazz bass lines and support a melody and or soloist.

Having covered the material in this book you are now well on your way to finding your own voice as a bassist and as a jazz musician.
Listen to as much music as you can, Listen to the masters.

NB. This book is designed to make the student familiar with reading and understanding chord symbols in a jazz context, therefore the use of enharmonics is applied.

The objective has been to make the material for the student as easy to absorb as possible, as a confidance building mechanism.

Your thoughts and comments are important to us and assist us in providing future generations of musicians with quality educational material.

Please send youre thoughts or comments to constructwalkingjazzbasslines@gmail.com

© Waterfall Publishing House 2010

Other books available in this series

PRINT EDITIONS

" Constructing Walking Jazz Bass Lines " Book I
Walking Bass Lines : The Blues in 12 Keys

" Constructing Walking Jazz Bass Lines " Book II
Walking Bass Lines : Rhythm Changes in 12 keys

" Constructing Walking Jazz Bass Lines " Book III
Walking Bass Lines : Standard Lines

" Constructing Walking Jazz Bass Lines " Book IV
Building a 12 key Facility for the Jazz Bassist

Bass Tablature Series

" Constructing Walking Jazz Bass Lines " Book I
Walking Bass Lines : The Blues in 12 Keys -Bass TAB Edition

" Constructing Walking Jazz Bass Lines " Book II
Walking Bass Lines : Rhythm Changes in 12 Keys - Bass TAB Edition

" Constructing Walking Jazz Bass Lines " Book III
Walking Bass Lines : Standard Lines - Bass TAB Edition

" Constructing Walking Jazz Bass Lines " Book IV
Bass Tab Edition - coming soon

E-BOOK EDITIONS

" Constructing Walking Jazz Bass Lines " Book I
Walking Bass Lines : The Blues in 12 Keys

"Constructing Walking Jazz Bass Lines " Book II
Walking Bass Lines : Rhythm Changes in 12 keys

" Constructing Walking Jazz Bass Lines " Book III
Walking Bass Lines : Standard Lines

© Waterfall Publishing House 2010

" Constructing Walking Jazz Bass Lines " Book IV
Building a 12 key Facility for the Jazz Bassist

Bass Tablature Series

" Constructing Walking Jazz Bass Lines " Book I
Walking Bass Lines : The Blues in 12 Keys -Bass TAB Edition

" Constructing Walking Jazz Bass Lines " Book II
Walking Bass Lines : Rhythm Changes in 12 Keys - Bass TAB Edition

" Constructing Walking Jazz Bass Lines " Book III
Walking Bass Lines : Standard Lines - Bass Tab Edition

" Constructing Walking Jazz Bass Lines " Book IV
Bass Tab Edition - coming soon

Follow us on the web for news and new release updates.

http://waterfallpublishinghouse.com

http://constructingwalkingjazzbasslines.com

http://basstab.net

Waterfall Publishing House is proud to be associated with the Trees for the Future Organisation. Visit them on the web at www.plant-trees.org .
Waterfall Publishing House will plant 1 tree per book sold in the " Constructing Walking Jazz Bass Lines " series through the " Trees for the Future " tree planting program and will match the commitment for a total of 2 trees planted per book sold.

Follow our quarterly progress at Waterfallpublishinghouse.com

© Waterfall Publishing House 2010

www.ingramcontent.com/pod-product-compliance
Lightning Source LLC
Chambersburg PA
CBHW080508110426
42742CB00017B/3034